Carnegie-Mellon University Press
Distributed by Columbia University Press
New York — Guilford, Surrey

©1979 Carnegie-Mellon University
Library of Congress Catalog Card Number 79-84801
ISBN Number 0-915604-33-7

The
1978
Benjamin F.
Fairless
Memorial
Lectures

Ideals
in
Collision

The
Relationship
between
Business
& the
News Media Rawleigh Warner Jr. & Leonard S. Silk

The Benjamin F. Fairless Memorial Lectures endowment fund has been established at Carnegie-Mellon University to support an annual series of lectures. An internationally known figure from the world of business, government, or education is invited each year to present three lectures at Carnegie-Mellon under the auspices of its Graduate School of Industrial Administration. In general, the lectures will be concerned with some aspects of business or public administration; the relationships between business and government, management and labor; or a subject related to the themes of preserving economic freedom, human liberty, and the strengthening of individual enterprise — all of which were matters of deep concern to Mr. Fairless throughout his career.

Mr. Fairless was president of United States Steel Corporation for fifteen years, and chairman of the board from 1952 until his retirement in 1955. A friend of Carnegie-Mellon University for many years, he served on the board of trustees from 1952 until his death. In 1959 he was named honorary chairman of the board.

Mr. Fairless died January 1, 1962

Rawleigh Warner, Jr., is chairman of the board of directors and chief executive officer of Mobil Corporation.

Under his leadership, Mobil has earned a reputation as an outspoken corporate citizen through a series of weekly editorial page advertisements in the nation's most respected newspapers, including *The New York Times.*

Mr. Warner joined Mobil in 1953 as assistant to the financial director of Socony Vacuum Overseas Supply Company. In 1956 he became assistant treasurer in the newly formed Mobil Overseas Supply Company, and later that year, was named manager of Mobil's economics department. He became manager of the Middle East Affairs Department in 1958.

When Mobil International Oil Company was formed in 1959, Mr. Warner was named regional vice president for the Middle East. He became executive vice president of Mobil International in 1960, and president in 1963.

One year later, he was elected a director, executive vice president and member of the executive committee of Mobil Oil Corporation, responsible for two operating divisions, Mobil International and Mobil Petroleum Company, Inc. He became president of Mobil Oil at the beginning of 1965, and chairman and chief executive officer in 1969.

In 1976, he became chairman of a new holding company — Mobil Corporation — while continuing to serve in the same capacities with Mobil Oil Corporation. The holding company, formed following shareholder approval, is the parent unit of the Mobil organization.

Mr. Warner is a director of American Telephone and Telegraph Company, American Petroleum Institute, Caterpillar Tractor Company, Chemical New York Corporation and Chemical Bank, American Express Company and the American Express International Banking Company, and National Council for United States-China trade. He is a trustee of the Woodrow Wilson International Center for Scholars.

He is chairman of Princeton University's Council for University Resources and a member of The Business Council, the Labor-Management Group, and the Business Roundtable Policy Committee.

In 1975 Mr. Warner received the National Brotherhood Award of the National Conference of Christians and Jews for "distinguished service in the field of human relations." In 1976 he received the honorary degree of Doctor of Commercial Science from Pace University and Pace's "Leader in Management" award. In 1977 he received the Boys' Clubs of America's Herbert Hoover Memorial award.

Leonard S. Silk is an economic columnist for *The New York Times.* Prior to joining *The Times* in 1970, he was a Senior Fellow at The Brookings Institution (1969), and had been with *Business Week* from 1954 to 1969, serving as editorial page editor and chairman of the editorial board from 1967.

Mr. Silk was educated at the University of Wisconsin where he received his A.B. in 1940 and went on to get his Ph.D. at Duke University in 1947. He was an economics instructor at both Duke University (1941-42) and the University of Maine (1947-48); an assistant professor of economics at Simmons College (1948-50); lecturer at New York University (1955-56), and Columbia University (1962-63); and Ford Foundation Distinguished Visiting Research Professor at Carnegie-Mellon University (1965-66). He served as a member of the President's Commission on Budget Concepts (1966-67). He is a member of the American Economic Association, a Fellow of the National Association of Business Economists, and a member of the Council on Foreign Relations. He was recently awarded an honorary Doctor of Laws degree by Duke University.

Mr. Silk has written several books, contributed to many others, and received various honors, including the Loeb Award for Distinguished Business and Financial Journalism in 1961, 1966, 1967, 1971, 1972, and 1977, and the Overseas Press Club Award for best business reporting from abroad in 1972. His most recent books are *Contemporary Economics; Nixonomics; Capitalism: The Moving Target; The Economists; Ethics and Profits: The Crisis of Confidence in American Business;* and *Economics in Plain English.*

The
1978
Benjamin F.
Fairless
Memorial
Lectures

Ideals
in
Collision

The Relationship between Business & the News Media

Ideals in Collision: The Relationship between Business and the News Media

by
Rawleigh Warner, Jr.
Chairman, Mobil Corporation

As the decade of the 1970s got under way, the political land-scape of the United States contained a major anomaly.

Labor unions which had long been active in politics, had attained a considerable degree of sophistication, at least at the federal level.

The same could be said of the farmers.

So-called "public interest" groups of a wide variety had arisen, had developed highly effective tactics, and — largely through skillful manipulation of television and the press — had attained political power out of all proportion to their numbers.

Other particularized constituencies were active, some of them focusing on only one issue (gun control, for instance, or educa-tion).

Yet private business, one of the major institutions in the coun-try and the source of the wealth that supported most of the other groups, had no really effective voice in matters of public policy.

In an unfortunate sort of way, this probably represented poetic justice. Business interests had pretty well dominated the country in the second half of the 19th century, particularly after the Second Industrial Revolution got under way following the Civil War, and through the first quarter or more of this century.

America's expansion across the continent — remember "Mani-fest Destiny" — was marked by the application of machine power, in constantly enlarged units, to new processes and new regions. The open and unlimited continent, and a public attuned to the rhythms of an agrarian age, were relatively easy prey. And the group that ultimately became known as the "robber barons" preyed on both.

While a useful by-product of the work of the robber barons was the opening up of a continent, the industrialization of a nation, and the creation of a national market — no mean accomplishment itself — their excesses understandably and properly led to government regulation of business, beginning with the Interstate Commerce Act of 1887. The rest is, of course, history. Regulation was piled on top of regulation, as political activists made almost a hobby of the process, and their zeal is still undiminished to this day.

Business was pilloried in the 1930s because it had failed to do what people expected it to do. Business became a favorite target, a scapegoat *par excellence*, and substantial change was wrought at its expense. It did little to help itself in the court of public opinion. Most leaders of business were still struggling to adapt to a new era while endeavoring to work out of the Great Depression. Many of them blindly opposed even the most needed reforms.

During most of this time — until quite recently, in fact — most business leaders felt their job was to run their businesses, and *not* to involve themselves publicly, since none of them wanted to attract the lightning. This did little to help them, as political demagogues in and out of government profited handsomely from business leaders' ineptitude in the rough-and-tumble of gut-issue politics.

Happily, there is now at least the beginning of a realization in our country that the pendulum has swung too far in the irrational bias against business. There seems to be a growing awareness that public policy has been tilted too much toward consumption as against investment . . . that business profits have been in a long-term decline as a proportion of Gross National Product . . . that capital formation on the scale required to create the number of jobs the country needs is facing a real crunch . . . that only a prosperous private sector can underpin American society.

One of the major reasons for this awareness of the need to redress the counterproductive imbalance has been the increasing participation of business leaders in the resolution of political issues. Today many members of top management realize increasingly that they have to be willing and able to engage in the give-and-take of ideas and viewpoints, on Capitol Hill and elsewhere.

Today's chief executive officer in particular must be a public figure, like it or not. He has to be willing to assume all of the risks and all of the headaches that this involves, no matter how uncomfortable he may be in that arena. The corporation's image can be humanized only by members of its top management — and the nearer the top, the better. Business leaders must play a continuing role in the formulation of public policy; otherwise they will fall victim to misguided policies.

An important element in inducing business leaders to join the fray has been an organization called the Business Roundtable. This group, dating from the early part of 1972, consists of the chief executive officers of some 190 firms. It was formed by a number of concerned individuals in business who felt it necessary to construct a mechanism whereby business could make its voice heard. They realized that the only effective way to do this was to involve the chief executive officers directly. This they have done.

The Roundtable makes no pretense of being *the* voice of American business; there are many voices, often quite divergent in their views on issues of public policy. Such success as the Roundtable has achieved has stemmed in large part from a high degree of selectivity in choosing and developing issues that are in the *public* interest as much as in its own. It has then translated these issues into carefully thought-out positions. Finally, chief executive officers of member companies have communicated these positions to people in government *personally*.

We in Mobil are encouraged by how successful the Roundtable has been. Business has begun to make its voice heard, which is all we really want. Those of us in the Roundtable cannot claim to have won every political fight we have taken on in Washington; we never expected to. But we *have* gotten a hearing for our views. We have presented factual, responsible — even scholarly — analyses of public issues and pending legislation. And we have had some moderating effect even when we have "lost" a fight.

Perhaps coincidentally, the country is seeing a resurgence of objective intellectual activity on college campuses that is producing numbers of young people not weighted down with the biases so evident only a few years ago. Research organizations such as the American Enterprise Institute have taken on stature and even luster.

None of which is to say the battle is anywhere near won. It is only to say that a wider spectrum of information and viewpoints is being made available to the body politic on important issues of public policy. It seems to us in business that this is essential to the formulation of informed decisions on what can be life-and-death issues for a nation.

Mobil's Advocacy Advertising

Mobil Corporation, while involving itself in the Business Roundtable and in ancillary activities, has been conducting an unusual activity of its own. Unusual and possibly unique.

I refer to what is known as "idea" advertising or "advocacy" advertising on a regular, continuing basis, year-in, year-out. We also refer to it in-house as "op-ed" advertising, since it began (and continues) on the page opposite the editorial page in *The New York Times*, though it has since been extended to include several other leading newspapers.

A word of background is in order.

By the time Mobil placed its first op-ed advertisement in *The Times*, in the fall of 1970, it had become clear to us that our country was heading for a severe energy crunch. Here was the greatest industrial power in the world, with its entire economy — indeed its whole way of life — built on an abundance of inexpensive energy, about to enter an era of more-expensive energy and unnecessarily heavy reliance on other countries. Oil and natural gas were, as they still are, our prime sources of energy.

The main reason for this crunch was misguided public policy over many years, as a result of which the petroleum industry was not being allowed to develop our very strong domestic energy resource potential adequately. There seemed little understanding of this situation or of the economics of business in the press, in the Congress, or among the general public. We in Mobil felt there was an urgent need — as much in the country's interest as in our own — to try to inform people.

Easier said than done, of course. As both technology and the reach of government have grown apace, it has become increasingly difficult for the average citizen to understand issues of public policy in any great depth. This seemed particularly true when technology or economics was involved, and doubly so when both were involved. Yet we knew that if we in private business were to retain our franchises, we had better recognize that the situation placed a special obligation on us to share our particular knowledge with the public to help it understand some of these complex issues. Additionally, we felt that Mobil was a distinctive company with its own distinctive personality and value patterns, and we wanted to convey this.

We therefore stopped cursing the darkness and lit our own modest candle.

We had no hope of being able to reach the public at large. The cost would have been prohibitive, even for a corporation as large as ours. So we opted to aim at an admittedly small cut of the public — the movers and shakers who are often called opinion-makers. These included, but were not limited to, business leaders, people in important positions in government, reporters and editors in all the communications media, members of the "Establishment," intellectuals. We felt that these people were best able to grasp complex issues and accustomed to dealing with ideas and with serious written material.

The op-ed space in *The Times* — a quarter-page in the lower right-hand corner of the op-ed page — is particularly attractive to us. It is the only advertising space sold on those two facing pages, so it commands attention. And those are the two pages to which our target audience turns early in its reading of that newspaper.

We decided at the outset that our material had to take the form of essays, urbane in nature and at least as literate and readable as the other material in that part of the paper. We decided also to go for the long term, since we knew it might take two or three years to establish ourselves and build the necessary rapport with the people we wanted to reach. We knew our advertisements would have to be, above all, accurate and responsible, because we intended from the beginning to deal with complex and difficult issues.

All this and other reasons persuaded us that this advertising would have to be written in-house by members of our own staff, who understood the oil business as well as business in general. And so it has been — every line of it, throughout.

In these "advocacy" advertisements, we have tried to surprise readers with our selection of subject matter, our headlines, and our brisk and often irreverent text. While, as I said, we seek a tone of urbanity, we eschew pomposity. We try not to talk to ourselves, and we accept that we can never say all we'd like to say about everything in any one advertisement. We try not to lecture, but rather to help people understand what options are open to them and what sorts of costs are involved in various trade-offs.

These essays of ours have ranged over a wide gamut — the energy problem in its many ramifications, the role of profits in American society, earnings expressed not only in absolute terms but also as a rate of return, capital requirements and capital formation, the need for a rational and comprehensive national energy policy (as urgent today as the beginning of this decade) . . . our reasons for supporting such institutions as the New York Public Library, the United Negro College Fund, the Legal Aid Society, the Better Business Bureau, public broadcasting (of which more later), and our hope that others also would support them . . . the need for continued economic growth . . . the dangers of simplistic knee-jerk reactions as the substitute for responsible policy-making . . . the need to conserve energy (beginning long before the crisis of 1973-74). The list is a long one.

We appear to have been the first, or in any event among the first, to urge that *economic* impact statements as well as *environmental* impact statements be made mandatory in the consideration of construction projects. An economic impact statement would spell out the effects on the economy of *not* going ahead with the project — such effects as the tax revenue lost, the number of jobs denied, the numbers of families thereby forced on welfare or kept there, and the number of children thus prevented from attending college.

When we have felt it necessary, we have taken on the Congress, the President, *The New York Times* (with which we joust rather frequently, in fact), and commercial television. Our practice has been to strike back quickly, forcibly, and factually.

The response from a wide variety of people to our op-ed advertisements in *The Times,* coupled with the increasing gravity of the situation as the nation drifted — understandably, perhaps, few Congressmen like to look more than two years ahead — led us to begin publishing these advertisements in a number of additional newspapers. The number has fluctuated. During the worst of the political demagoguery attending the Arab oil embargo of 1973-74, with suddenly increased prices and long lines at service stations in some parts of the country, we ran our advocacy advertising in slightly more than 100 newspapers each week. (Those with long memories will recall charges made in the halls of Congress of "obscene" profits by oil companies, and allegations — eventually disproved, of course — that the oil crisis was rigged by the oil companies.)

Our weekly op-ed advertisements currently appear in *The New York Times, the Boston Globe, the Washington Post, the Washington Star, the Los Angeles Times, the Chicago Tribune,* and all editions of the *Wall Street Journal.* The list is, of course, subject to rapid expansion on very short notice.

The Carter Energy Plan and Mobil's Response

It will be recalled that during 1977 the Administration rammed its so-called energy bill through the House of Representatives, which hardly laid a glove on it. This 500-odd-page piece of legislation sailed through in record time, with minimal hearings. Unfortunately for the Administration, the Senate took the time to read the proposed legislation, recoiled in some horror, and decided to hold the sort of extensive public hearings that such fundamental legislation required.

Mobil set forth its views on the President's so-called energy program in its op-ed advertisements and also in a number of full-page advertisements in leading newspapers across the country. In brief, our objections to the President's proposals were and are these:

• In essence, it discouraged or forbade just about everything that was needed while encouraging precisely the wrong things.

• It was not an energy bill at all, but a tax bill, an administrative nightmare, and a plan for redistribution of wealth through the largest tax increase ever proposed in peacetime.

• While quite properly urging conservation, the program was dangerously unbalanced, because conservation alone simply cannot do the whole job. What is needed along with it is greatly increased production of secure domestic energy.

• The Administration's proposals did not contain enough incentives to bring forth the large-scale exploration effort the country needs, and on this point the simple truth is that the President and Secretary Schlesinger still have not focused publicly on the supply side of the equation.

• The President's program revealed an unwillingness to recognize the existing environmental restraints on coal and nuclear power.

• Finally, the Administration proposed not only to continue the federal price controls on interstate natural gas that have created a totally unnecessary shortage of this attractive and versatile fuel, but to compound the fiasco by extending the same sort of price controls to natural gas that is consumed in the state where it is produced.

I cite these flaws — fatal flaws, in my considered opinion — to make it clear that Mobil's opposition to this so-called energy program was not automatic nor was it capricious. In fact, we held our fire initially, searching for elements in the plan that we could endorse. After all, we had for years been urging the formulation and adoption of sound U.S. energy policies. But the more we analyzed the Adminstration's energy proposals, the clearer it became to us that they not only were inadequate, but also added up to a recipe for disaster.

We therefore saw no alternative to opposing those proposals, and oppose them we have. In opposing them, however, we have sought to present reasoned analyses, including the dangers of ignoring the lead times characteristic of the energy industries. These lead times are so long that changing course cannot be accomplished overnight — or, indeed, even within three or four years. It can take from five to ten years or more to find oil or gas in a "frontier" area and to begin producing and refining it. It can take up to eight years to open a new underground coal mine; up to 12 years to construct a nuclear power plant and put it into operation.

Factor these lead times by the truly enormous amounts of energy the United States uses, and you can begin to see the hole in which misguided energy policies can put us, and indeed have already put us.

Our country has a potentially very strong energy resource base — sizeable amounts of oil and natural gas still to be discovered onshore and offshore; sizeable reserves of uranium; enough commercially recoverable coal to last 400 years at present rates of production; even larger volumes of oil locked in shale, though not without its own great environmental problems — not to mention, of course, solar and perhaps other exotic forms of energy eventually.

Mobil has for years pointed to the urgent need to develop this energy resource base. Three months after the President sent his energy proposals to Capitol Hill, we published a full-page advertisement in 11 major newspapers and in several news weeklies and other magazines, under a headline that read: "We'd like to challenge those who say we have to live with a long-term shortage of energy. We say there are ample energy resources. We say those who claim we have to live with shortages are creating and extending the very shortage they warn against."

The gist of that ad was (1) There really is no long-term shortage of energy in our country; the problem centers on the *deliverability* of energy from our energy resource base; and (2) we believe that Administration energy advisers have grossly over-estimated any negative social and economic consequences of the *development* of U.S. energy resources and have grossly *under*-estimated, or ignored altogether, the negative social and economic consequences of *non*-development. This is probably the greatest flaw in the President's energy proposals, and this alone would be enough to condemn his program.

I have commented this extensively on U.S. energy policy and on some of the many advertisements we have published concerning it simply to stress that we have sought to meet even the most complex and difficult issues head-on and that we have not done so out of spite, but rather after reasoned analysis.

As may be evident, our op-ed ads tend to be rather sophisticated, both in subject matter and in treatment. We reach a considerably larger audience across the country with somewhat less-complex material through a weekly advertisement — also in the form of a low-key, discursive essay — called "Observations." This appears in 470 newspapers and reaches nearly half of the households in the country. Additionally, we have published advertisements in various magazines.

We have published a number of what might be called "rebuttal" ads, particularly when we have felt that some of the reporting on our industry or our company was so inaccurate and misleading as to cry for a response.

The most recent example came on August 8, 1978, on the American Broadcasting Company's "20/20" television show. The show purported to analyze the natural gas bill then before the Congress and was so inaccurate we felt we had to respond.

After carefully studying tapes of the show, we were forced to the conclusion that those responsible for it simply had not read the legislation they were discussing; or that, if they had, they lacked either the desire or the ability to understand complex material; or were simply conducting a lynching party for the oil and gas industry through flagrant untruths couched in a demagogic presentation, including material taken out of context.

We found it a shocking spectacle, even for ABC. Because of our concern over the gross misrepresentations in the broadcast, Mobil offered to make a five-minute film at its own expense to correct the record — no opinion, only demonstrable facts; no position for or against the legislation. We asked the network to run such a film on "20/20" or to let us buy commercial time for it. ABC refused both requests, saying "ABC does not sell time for comment on controversial issues."

We asked ABC whether we could question Hugh Downs and

Sylvia Chase, the two prime purveyors of misinformation on the program. Certainly not, ABC said.

Mobil thereupon prepared a rebuttal that ran as a full-page ad in the *Wall Street Journal* and a two-page spread in various smaller-size newspapers, under the headline "ABC-TV's '20/20' needs its eyes examined." It was published a little over three weeks after that show was broadcast; careful, responsible analysis takes time, which may be why it often seems to have little attraction for the networks.

Our ad pointed out what we considered the worst of the specific untruths in that program and the shoddy lack of professionalism the show reflected.

Unlike "20/20," we limited ourselves to a factual analysis both of the pending legislation and of ABC's distortions of what the legislation did and did not provide for — point by point.

And we quoted a few of the country's television critics' comments on "20/20":

● John J. O'Connor, of *The New York Times*: "One of the more disturbing aspects of the program is a tendency to over-dramatize points, to clobber the viewer with emotional gimmicks . . . In addition to being pointless, the new ABC News Magazine (20/20) is dizzyingly absurd."

● Tom Shales, of the *Washington Post*: "Bubblegum news, as practiced . . . by ABC's '20/20' is information packaged like a Krazy Kat cartoon — anti-news designed not to pierce one's perceptions beyond a mere tickling of the eyeballs."

● William Hickey, the (Cleveland) *Plain Dealer*: "Talk about tawdry, cheap-shot journalism, the '20/20' mini-view of Cleveland was in a class by itself . . . The 14-minute piece was a preconceived and deftly executed hatchet job."

It is difficult to determine how effective such print advertisements as this one are in minimizing the damage done to a whole industry via television. The statistics we have indicate that millions who see such programs as "20/20" are not habitual readers of newspapers — are, in fact, not even habitual readers. But since the three commercial television networks enjoy such a dominant position, free flow of ideas in the United States would be severely crimped if it were not for the commitment by newspapers to the principle that a free society requires the broadest possible spectrum of information and viewpoints. So we resort to replying in print to television's misstatements, even if the audiences do not match up as precisely as we would like.

The Right to Advocacy Advertising

Mobil's advocacy advertising has, as one might expect, raised some basic questions: Does private business have any *right* to engage in a dialogue on issues of public policy, as Mobil does in such advertising? And if it has a *right*, does it also have an *obligation* to do so?

It is clear where Mobil comes out on these questions.

We have believed all along that under the First Amendment we have a clear-cut right to add our voice to those already being heard in the marketplace of ideas and democratic debate.

If democracy is to survive in our country, the people must be well-informed. Hence the necessity of what the Supreme Court has termed "uninhibited, robust, and wide-open" debate on public issues. The vitality of free institutions depends on public understanding and support, and these in turn depend on an abundance of accurate information and access to conflicting viewpoints. But access denied is access curtailed.

As Norman Cousins commented in an editorial in the *Saturday Review* — titled, interestingly enough, "A Fairness Doctrine for the Press?" — the danger is that "if the news is skewed or tilted or significantly incomplete, then the quality of decisions will be affected. The real issue, therefore, is not falsification but responsibility, not accuracy but decency."

We concur in Judge Learned Hand's statement that ". . . right conclusions are more likely to be gathered out of a multitude of tongues than through any kind of authoritative selection. To many this is, and always will be folly, but we have staked up on it our all."

The Supreme Court Decision in Bellotti

The U.S. Supreme Court unequivocally confirmed corporate freedom to speak in *First National Bank of Boston v. Bellotti,* better known as *Bellotti,* in the spring of 1978.

Mr. Justice Powell said in that decision that free speech ". . . is indispensable to decision-making in a democracy, and this is no less true because speech comes from a corporation rather than an individual . . . The inherent worth of speech in terms of its capacity for informing the public does not depend upon the identity of its source, whether a corporation, association, union, or individual."

Justice Powell said also, in *Bellotti,* ". . . the press does not have a monopoly on either the First Amendment or the ability to enlighten . . . In the realm of protected speech, the legislature is constitutionally disqualified from dictating the subjects about which persons may speak and the speakers who may address a public issue."

As Mr. Leonard Silk pointed out in *The New York Times* of May 25, "Mr. Burger in his *Bellotti* opinion does not seek to narrow the rights of the press but to broaden the rights of other corporations. If it is all right for the newspapers to do something, he seems to imply, it is all right for anyone else.

"The Burger opinion concludes that no factual distinction has been identified that would justify government restraints on corporations without, at the same time, 'opening the door to similar restraints on media conglomerates with their vastly greater influence.'"

The *Wall Street Journal* concluded an editorial on *Bellotti* with this:

"The notion that mere money to buy ads somehow 'tilts' power implies that after 200 years of democracy, the American electorate still is not fit to weigh all the various arguments and decide who comes up wanting . . . If everyone — even those artificial beings called corporations . . . has a say in public debate, public information and democracy can only benefit."

Thus clearly having the *right* to engage in advocacy advertising, we believe we also have *obligations* to do so — obligations to our employees, to our shareholders, to the general public. One has to ask himself, what is the posture of an industry that, even when seriously threatened, is unwilling to defend itself publicly? Who will come to our defense if we are not willing to stand up for ourselves? The answer, as everyone knows, is: Nobody.

One of the things that has created a threat to our industry, by making it a prime target for political demagoguery, has been the fact that the news media have been unable to provide adequate, and adequately informed, coverage of the energy situation. With all respect to the electronic media, as I shall develop later, they are primarily in the business of entertainment and are structurally unable to handle complex issues well on their news shows. And with all respect to the print media, they are as a whole still laboring to develop sufficient expertise to cover energy matters in any great depth. Newspapers, particularly, have shown improvement in this respect in the past four or five years, but many reporters and editors still have trouble understanding business in general well enough to report on it adequately.

A poll recently quoted by Dr. Edward J. Mitchell, professor of business economics at the University of Michigan, in the American Enterprise Institute's magazine, *Regulation*, is germane here: "A recent survey on competition in the oil industry showed that university professors who are economic experts on the industry hold views directly opposite to those of journalists on every issue of substance." The point Mobil has been trying to make ever since it initiated its advocacy advertising is that our problems with the press stem not from bias, but from ignorance.

As a privately owned business and more particularly as a large international oil company, Mobil has found that what we have to contend with is not only people who disagree with us — which is to be expected in a free society — but also people who do not understand the issues or who actually *mis*understand them. As the possessors of a considerable degree of expertise amassed around the world through a great many years, we believe we have a responsibility to inform both the press and the public, as well as the government, in areas where we think any of them is uninformed, or, worse, *mis*informed.

In our view, we have no practical alternative to speaking up publicly. We think it is no exaggeration to say we have to publish or perish, and we do not intend to perish if we can help it.

We believe also that shareholders expect more from corporate management today than just the ability to assess business opportunities and make sound operating decisions. We think they are beginning to look at a company's ability to anticipate political, social, and economic issues and to deal with those issues. We see shareholders and potential shareholders analyzing, as part of their investment decisions, how well — or how poorly — a company comprehends its environment and communicates with, and has impact on, the various publics that affect its destiny.

The Fear of Bigness and the Power of Size

I realize that some may fear that in the arena of advocacy advertising, large corporations will dominate the field. This strikes us as unlikely, for two main reasons: (1) The cost is modest enough for even relatively small businessess to afford; Mobil's outlay for space and production costs for its op-ed campaign in the seven papers mentioned earlier comes to only about $1.4 million a year. (2) There is no single voice in American business, even among the largest firms. There are many divergent views and voices, which is as it should be and is quite understandable if one stops to think about it. Our own view is that we wish *more* businesses were using this means of communication.

The truth is that by speaking out, business is only beginning to redress an obvious imbalance. Politicians who make anti-business statements have no difficulty breaking into print; their pontifications become "instant news," and they do not have to resort to the advertising columns. Nor do the self-proclaimed public interest groups, and others of an anti-business bent. Were business to receive as much attention in the news columns as its critics, its reliance on advocacy advertising would not be as pressing. If anything, it is the anti-business forces who manipulate the media.

One of the best examples of this manipulation is Sun Day 1978; even the media, we believe, now realize how they were exploited on this one. The general impression that Sun Day managed to leave with readers and viewers, in addition to free publicity for some entertainers, was that the only thing standing between the public and a limitless supply of clean, virtually free solar energy was the oppressive capitalistic system, particularly the big oil companies.

What about the power that sheer size appears to give corporations, power of which some people seem to stand in fear and awe?

This has led some to call for a "code of corporate ethics." In our view, a corporation consists entirely of individuals, and these individuals certainly must have strong personal ethics and a sense of responsibility to the public — humility, to use a rather tired word — if abuses are to be prevented. We believe the record will show that most business leaders do have such a sense of responsibility and that they do attempt to balance the private interest with the public good. It is the exceptions who make news, and the news they make is often treated in a way that seems to impute malefaction to all of us in business.

A statement by Tom Bethell, a Washington editor of *Harper's* magazine, quoted in a recent issue of *Newsweek* is pertinent: "What is surprising is that the far smaller public-interest lobbies should have succeeded in putting the vast majority on the defensive. They have done this by appearing in the guise not of self-interest lobbyists but of disinterested 'reformers,' roaming all over the political landscape to seek out 'conflict of interest,' which — by default — they alone define. We should bear in mind that such people have a 'vested interest' in persuading us that 'the system doesn't work.'"

A main reason it "doesn't work," they would have you believe, is that business has too much power and abuses that power through anti-social behavior. This is the drumbeat against which we have to work and to manage large organizations whose goods and services are essential to American society and to that of other countries.

Does Mobil draw any criticism for its advocacy advertising? Yes, some. We take some very controversial positions, for which we are occasionally denounced within our own industry. Among the larger public, a few maintain we are monopolizing the expression of viewpoints. This borders on the hilarious, on the face of it, and is particularly hard to understand if one recognizes the audience that will be reading our views in paid advertisements and reflects on this audience. It is bright, sophisticated, and has its own positions (by no means uniform) on issues. All we have ever tried to do is to get its attention in order to offer an additional viewpoint for consideration.

In trying to communicate with people who, though bright and well educated, do not always understand our business or even business itself very well, do we trivialize important matters? Certainly not consciously, and in my view not at all. We have first-rate professional economists and other specialists on our staff, for instance, and their help on our advertisements is valuable. The final product however, is addressed not to specialists in any field, but to a broader audience of opinion-makers.

Is our advocacy advertising a cover-up, a way of avoiding the tough questions a reporter would ask in an interview? Hardly. We talk freely to reporters. Each week we have an on-the-record lunch at our headquarters in New York, at which our guests may come from any of the communications media — individuals ranging from John Chancellor, Harry Reasoner, and Walter Cronkite, representing television news, to daily newspapers and wire-service reporters and editors and to magazines and trade publications. I see a good many reporters, from this country, the Far East, and Europe, in the course of a year. Mobil directors have frequently gone out across the country to subject themselves to lengthy and searching interviews by reporters from newspapers and from television and radio — live and unrehearsed.

Once we talk to a reporter, we have no control and in fact not even any influence over how he treats that information. We respect the fact that reporters and editors and their superiors have their own ideas and their own positions and can put *our* views into *their* context. We keep coming back to this basic point: We just want to avoid being misunderstood or ignored, because we believe that what we have to say is at least worth hearing or reading.

A Conservative View of Tax-Deductibility

A word about the deductibility of our advocacy advertisements as a business expense is in order. To put it briefly, we have always made it a point to be on the side of the angels in this respect.

By way of background, U.S. Treasury regulations state clearly that expenditures for "institutional or 'goodwill' advertising" are generally deductible as part of the cost of doing business. Additionally, the Treasury says advertising expenditures are tax-deductible if the advertising "presents views on economic, financial, social or other subjects of a general nature," provided that they do not include expenditures for lobbying for promotion or defeat of legislation, or for related propaganda.

Mobil submits *all* of its advertisements to outside counsel for its opinion on their tax-deductibility, and counsel has instructions to adopt a conservative standard in determining deductibility under the statutes, regulations, and case law on the subject. This decision to take a conservative view of what constitutes tax-deductibility has obviously cost us money.

We take this extremely conservative view of what constitutes tax-deductibility in the belief that fundamental issues of national concern are at stake, and we feel we would do both ourselves and the country a disservice by losing sight of them. The country needs a free marketplace of ideas and opinions and it desperately needs the sort of coherent, productive national energy policy that can develop only when the people have the facts and can make balanced, informed judgments on the issues.

This matter of deductibility raises the question of whether newspapers deduct — or should be allowed to deduct — as business expenses the cost of producing their editorial pages, or at least those portions of their editorial pages that advocate legislative action or non-action by government at some level. This is not to quibble over tax deductions per se, but rather to raise the question of whether enforcement of the tax laws is equal and even handed.

Why should Mobil's messages be subject to greater scrutiny by tax authorities than those of the media corporations? If a media conglomerate publishes an editorial in favor of a given piece of legislation or other proposed action by government, it may well be doing so to protect the interests of one of its non-publishing operations. In Mobil's case, we would rule such a message non-deductible.

What basis is there for treating the costs or legality of published endorsements of political candidates by media corporations differently from those of non-media corporations? Indeed, such distinctions blur when one looks at an organization such as the New York Times Company, whose interests now include timber, pulp, and paper products, several magazines, and book publishing.

To repeat, our chief concern is not with the tax aspect itself, but rather with the chilling effect that unequal enforcement of the tax rules, and singling out various business groups for special scrutiny, can have on the public's right to information from a wide variety of sources. As Mr. Justice Powell said in *Bellotti*, ". . . the First Amendment does not 'belong' to any definable category of persons or entities; it belongs to all who exercise its freedoms."

The Impact of Mobil's Advocacy Advertising

Has Mobil's advocacy advertising been worth the time and effort?

All in all, there is reason to believe that our print advertisements over the past seven or eight years have had some impact. The response has been strong and generally favorable, though it must be remembered that in addressing ourselves mainly to opinion leaders, we have deliberately opted for a rather thin cut of the total public. We seem to have been reaching people other than just those already wedded to the free market. We have had a particularly strong response from educators, in this country and abroad. They and others have requested literally tens of thousands of copies of some of the series we have printed in booklet form and have offered free of charge — most notably one called "Toward a Healthier Economic Climate." We continue to receive requests for reprints of our advertisements almost daily, and we are happy to honor them.

One reason we think they may be having some effect, along with those of other oil companies, is that several Congressmen and Senators have tried to inhibit us. We believe the *Wall Street*

Journal was close to the target when it said, "Indeed, the reason the critics are rushing to have them gagged is that the oil companies have been making legitimate arguments worthy of being heard."

Viewing it from our corporate vantage point, we have the conviction that we are listened to and in many ways respected even if not necessarily loved, and we have never deluded ourselves that any large corporation would be loved. We get a good deal of favorable playback — along, of course, with some static — from Capitol Hill and various regulatory agencies in Washington. Even during our sustained opposition to the Administration's energy plan, particularly in 1977, we had comments from people in the White House who deal in this area that they respected what Mobil was doing and hoped we and they could find common ground.

I think it is fair to say that our employees and annuitants are particularly enthusiastic about this advertising. They know the facts about our business, and their morale seems to be lifted when they see the company hitting back at obvious misstatements of fact, even when made by the President. I would guess that many of our shareholders feel pretty much the same way.

We get a good deal of mail approving of the stands we take and the way we express our views — and, of course, a few choice denunciations along the way.

Something that Louis Banks, a former managing editor of *Fortune* magazine, said in the *Harvard Business Review* about Mobil's advocacy advertising seems relevant here:

> Subtle shifts in editorial points of view are all but impossible to measure if only because they usually are shrouded in claims of consistency, but I myself believe that the tone of many columnists and editorialists changed under the factual barrage. In discussions of energy matters, the bellwether *New York Times,* for one, revealed its awareness of the terse, newsy arguments in the small Mobil advertisements tucked into the corner of its op-ed page.

> What Mobil and others are proving is that it is possible for individual corporations or industries to take part in the argument about specific issues *on behalf of the public interest,* and thus gain media attention (if not affection) and a chance for the public to make up its mind from a broader set of arguments.

Certainly the survival of a pluralistic society demands that every point of view be able to express itself, no matter how abhorrent some views may be to some people — even to the majority — and to some institutions. With all due respect to newspapers and magazines and to their professed view that they are the surrogates of the public — and this seems particulary true of newspapers — they, too, have vested interests and they, too, have points of view, which is healthy.

There is no reason they should not express their views freely, even when those views appear to rest on "information" that does not stand up to informed scrutiny. Mobil, like many other corporations, has a point of view that differs from that of many newspapers, and we believe we have the right to present it. The public has both the right and the need to be exposed to all these various, and frequently conflicting, points of view.

In the final analysis, it seems to us that one has to stand for something. One has to live with himself, and we in Mobil are at least getting the satisfaction of knowing that in our own way we are explaining and defending business and the American system of democratic capitalism. We believe this system is preeminently worth defending — not because it's perfect, which it certainly is not, but because we have seen every other sort of system tried in one country or another around the world, and they all come off second best.

As indicated earlier, when we began our advocacy advertising in the fall of 1970, we opted for print media because this was the medium in which we felt we could best develop our points adequately and because the audience at which we were aiming was one that habitually looked to print media for intellectual interest and sustenance.

We were to find out the hard way the our choice had actually been made for us.

Structural Deficiences of Network Television News

When the energy crisis hit full-blown in the fall of 1973, there were few reporters in any medium anywhere in the country, outside of oil-producing areas and the oil trade press, who knew much about oil. This was, and is, particularly true of commercial network television. There appear to be at least five major elements that account for the structural deficiency of network television news programs.

The first is time limitations. A 30-minute news program, such as the Cronkite show, shrinks after commercials to around 23 to 24 minutes. An essay by some commentator such as a Sevareid, now retired, or a Brinkley, can consume around three minutes, leaving only 20 to 21 minutes for news. The show will often try to cover 15 or more items, the biggest of which may consume close to two minutes each. So a good many stories get handled in well *under* a minute each. Also, topical stories for the evening news usually have to be filmed by noon or shortly after noon, which leads to the creation — and broadcast — of "media events."

Second, there are the economic limitations. Camera crews are expensive. The cost of trying to keep them in many different locations could be prohibitive. This often imposes prior limitations on what viewers will see.

The third structural limitation has to do with the networks' seeming compulsion to personalize the news in their ever-present need for the highest rating. Size of audience becomes paramount, with the result that balanced presentation of the news is subordinated to personalities and showmanship.

Here is what Fred W. Friendly, the Edward R. Morrow professor of broadcast journalism at Columbia University and one of the most distinguished observers of television in the country, said about this in *The New York Times* on Sunday, August 6, 1978: "The most serious threat to television and its claim to First Amendment freedoms is not the Federal Communications Commission or the Supreme Court or an Imperial Presidency, but the runaway television rating process."

The fourth of the elements that tend to emasculate network news is personnel limitations. There appears to be little room for specialists, except for sports announcers and weather forecasters. Understandably, perhaps, most TV news correspondents are generalists competent to cover hard-news stories of many kinds, but usually severely limited in the spheres of economics, finance, and technology.

The fifth weakness is simply that by its very nature television is an entertainment medium, and a highly visual one at that. The problem was summed up this way by a former president of NBC News: "Every news story should, without any sacrifice of probity or responsibility, display the attributes of fiction, or drama. It should have structure and conflict, problem and denouement, rising action and falling action, a beginning, a middle, and an end."

Because oil companies deal in such large volumes and deploy

such substantial assets as to make even modest earnings seem enormous to the uninformed, we start out with an almost unsurmountable problem in trying to convey even the simplest facts to the public. And when we have to cope with TV reporters and commentators who know next to nothing about the business and seldom seem to have the time or the desire to learn, we are in a very difficult position indeed.

Networks Reject Mobil's Advocacy Commercials

In late 1973 and early 1974, with millions of angry Americans queued up at service stations trying to buy gasoline and with something close to national hysteria having been whipped up, mainly by television, Mobil endeavored to buy air time for television commercials that would convey our point of view — commercials that would deal in ideas rather than in products. The networks rejected nearly all of the commercials we submitted.

The networks' position was pretty well summed up in a letter of February 27, 1973, from the law department of the Columbia Broadcasting System to a vice president of Mobil, that contained this statement: ". . . .it is the general policy of CBS to sell time only for the promotion of goods and services, not for the presentation of points of view on controversial issues of public importance. CBS has adopted this policy because it believes that the public will best be served if important public issues are presented in formats determined by broadcast journalists."

In simple terms, what this means is that what the people of this country see and hear on commercial television is to be decided largely by a very few people at each of three television networks.

It occurred to us that the networks might be afraid they would have to give free air time to opponents of our viewpoints. We therefore offered to pay *twice* the going rate to have our commercials telecast, which would have covered the cost of any free time given to someone with different views to reply to us — Ralph Nader, the Sierra Club, or anyone else selected by the network. Mark that: to be selected by the network, not by us.

We felt this underscored our basic posture: that we are not seeking to alter what the TV networks broadcast under the name of news. We just want to offer a broader spectrum of information and viewpoints to the public and are perfectly willing to take our chances in the marketplace of ideas. If our ideas are not good, the public will most assuredly shoot them down, and deservedly.

The networks have refused to sell us time even on this basis, yet have permitted our critics — mostly self-seeking politicians and ambitious "public interest" spokesmen — to keep up a stream of unsubstantiated charges against us and to get their views televised almost at will.

We set out in the spring of 1974 to produce possibly the blandest, most innocuous commercial ever made, to test the networks. It opens, without narration, on a shot of beach and ocean. Then as the camera moves out to show only the sea, the narrator comes in, and here is his entire script, verbatim:

According to the U.S. Geological Survey, there may be more oil beneath our continental shelf than this country has consumed in its entire history.

Some people say we should be drilling for that oil and gas. Other say we shouldn't because of the possible environmental risks. We'd like to know what you think.

Write Mobil Poll, Room 647, 150 East 42nd Street, New York 10017. We'd like to hear from you.

NBC accepted this commercial, without change.

ABC rejected it, on May 23, 1974, saying it had reviewed the commercial and was "unable to grant an approval for use over our facilities." No reason given.

CBS also rejected it, also on May 23, saying, "We regret that this message addresses a controversial issue of public importance and as such cannot be addressed under our corporate policies."

Interesting.

Interesting and worrisome.

This country was founded in controversy — hard, honest, openly expressed controversy — and it has remained free and democratic through the continuing clash of opinion and of value patterns. Television's gag confines that medium to superficial treatment of the issues of our time, avoidance of controversy, and refusal of responses.

If the networks dedicate themselves almost exclusively to merchandising products, via the entertainment route, they may raise serious questions as to whether what they merchandise as news is actually just entertainment.

When as powerful and pervasive a medium as television will not sell time for controversial issues, it seems to me our country has reached a rather critical juncture. How can a democracy operate effectively without broad public access to clashing points of view?

It is worth recalling what the U.S. Supreme Court said in 1969, in what is known as the Red Lion case: "It is the right of viewers and listeners, not the right of the broadcasters, which is paramount. It is the purpose of the First Amendment to preserve an uninhibited marketplace of ideas in which truth will ultimately prevail, rather than to countenance the monopolization of that market, whether it be by the government itself or by a private licensee. It is the right of the public to receive suitable access to social, political, esthetic, moral, and other ideas and experiences which is crucial here."

We in Mobil obviously do not believe the commercial television networks have made an adequate effort to provide such access. This becomes clear when one contrasts their position to that of newspapers. Most daily newspapers have developed a structure for obtaining and printing a wide spectrum of information and viewpoints. In addition to news and feature stories, they carry editorials and letters to the editor. Many, like *The New York Times*, have op-ed pages, where a wide variety of guest writers present many different points of view.

Additionally, of course, newspapers sell advertising space, where corporations such as Mobil have the opportunity to present their own views — views that often are radically different from those of the newspapers in which they appear. This practice does not appear to have caused any problems for those newspapers. On the contrary, they appear to be delighted to receive those advertisements and in the process to broaden the spectrum of viewpoints available to their readers, which is one of their responsibilities to the public.

A final comment on that bland, innocuous commercial that ABC and CBS rejected: We published it as a print ad in *The New York Times*, reproducing both its visual content and complete text,and asked people to write and give us their opinions on this issue of free speech. We received more than 2,000 written replies, in short order, overwhelmingly in favor of our right to express our viewpoint on the air.

Before leaving the subject of commercial televison networks, it should be pointed out that Mobil has had considerably better luck in its relations with *local* TV stations across the country — and, for that matter, with local radio stations as well. These local stations seem more receptive to facts, in our experience. Certainly they have broadcast many editorials eminently fair to the oil industry and to business as a whole.

Mobil's Support of Public Broadcasting

In quite a different vein, we also have had a happy and rewarding relationship with *public* broadcasting, to which we have given substantial support — relatively large in financial terms and unusual, if not in fact unique, in its nature.

We wanted to help public broadcasting in its effort to continue improving the quality and range of its programming, and we wanted to help build a larger audience for it and consequently a larger base of financial support. In our activities in this connection, we have sought not only to underwrite programs of the first order of quality, such as "Upstairs, Downstairs," but also to utilize our own corporate resources and skills to build a wider audience.

One must keep in mind that corporate executives live on the same planet as their critics, and in a world that has been endowed by centuries of theater, opera, music, and literature. We at Mobil seek to bring new enrichment to the society that so nurtures us, and we think that people are becoming increasingly intolerant of institutions that fail to do so.

We do not believe that, as a company, we exist by divine right. We exist within society, deriving our right to do so by our usefulness to that society. In enriching our society and the best of its values, we believe we help to invigorate the environment in which we function as a business.

It seems to us in Mobil that the United States, and perhaps much of the rest of the world as well, has entered a period in which people will increasingly want to know more about a corporation than just the quality of its products. We believe that from here on, larger and larger numbers of people will want to know something of the basic beliefs and value patterns of those who make up the top management of large corporations and who inevitably exert impact on society.

We are persuaded that in the long term our company can function best in an environment nurturing, and nurtured by, the arts. The alternative would be a barren environment, deficient in the humanities and almost totally materialistic.

All of this predisposition pointed us in favor of public television, which lives not by ratings alone. We felt confident there were millions of Americans eager for the sort of fare proposed by public television — if only someone put enough muscle into advertising and promotion to reach them, to get them to test the water. We decided to do just this even before we initiated "Masterpiece Theatre," at the beginning of 1971.

Over and above all the customary tools, we were able to utilize avenues of promotion not open to every company — 25,000 service station dealers across the country, 200,000 shareholders, several million credit-card holders, and of course our own employees and annuitants in the United States and Canada. All in addition to buying a good deal of advertising space in newspapers and magazines, and special promotion efforts directed to high school and college students. Not to mention paying for publicity tours in the U.S. by various of the stars of "Upstairs, Downstairs," who appeared on talk shows of all sorts and were interviewed by the print press.

While promotion of *commercial* television may have reached these levels before, we apparently were the first to put this much effort behind *public* television.

We have tried throughout to underwrite top-flight programs on public television, but we have never gone only for sure winners. On the contrary, we have underwritten some dramas — by Tolstoi and Dostoevski, for instance — simply because the Public Broadcasting Service felt they were important and deserved to be seen, even though many people might find them heavy going.

A good deal of fan mail and many awards, including more than 40 Emmy nominations and about half that many Emmy awards, have come our way via "Masterpiece Theatre" and other outstanding series we have underwritten,such as Jacob Bronowski's "The Ascent of Man;" "War and Peace;" "Decades of Decision: The American Revolution;" "Classic Theatre — The Humanities in Drama" (including "Macbeth," "The Duchess of Malfi," "She Stoops to Conquer," "Candide," "The Playboy of the Western World," and others); and, more recently, Ben Wattenberg's "In Search of the Real America."

During the eight years since Mobil began underwriting "Masterpiece Theatre," there has been a sizeable increase in the amount of corporate underwriting for public television and in individual contributions to help support local public broadcasting stations. If Mobil has been a catalytic factor in this, we are glad, but there remains a crying need for even greater financial support of this medium.

Questions have been raised as to the propriety of corporate support of public broadcasting. Mobil for one does not want to see public broadcasting become overly dependent on any single source of support — least of all the government. In our view, that would undermine the independence that is the heart of its vitality and its future.

Here is what John Jay Iselin, president of public broadcasting station WNET (Channel 13) in New York, has to say on this subject: "Interference is a very real danger from any source that provides money. But we have no experience with corporate sponsors trying to encroach, and we have a lot of experience with the Federal Government saying how public television should administer itself and direct its funds . . . The limited partnership with the business community is healthy for noncommercial broadcasting."

Our own experience in working with public broadcasting has been a pleasant one on the whole, possibly because we have had so few requests to make. We believe it is fair to say that neither of us has sought to corrupt the other; indeed the ground rules would hardly make that possible. Under those rules a company is entitled only to the briefest sort of credit for underwriting a particular program or series; that is all there is, and that is all there should be.

In our minds, Mobil's support of public broadcasting (and other cultural activities to which we contribute) is all of a piece with our outspoken support of the American system of democratic capitalism. We are convinced that if our economic system is destroyed or fatally weakened by the relatively few but highly articulate elitists who seem bent on doing just that — all in the name of progress and democracy, of course, and whether from ignorance or whatever motivation — then our democratic society and our cultural institutions will be imperiled.

In its offerings on commercial television, Mobil has sought on a modest scale to carry over the high level of quality that has characterized its participation in public broadcasting. Our commercial programs have included "Ceremonies in Dark Old Men," "Robinson Crusoe," "Queen of the Stardust Ballroom," "A Moon for the Misbegotten," "Ten Who Dared," "The Entertainer," "Minstrel Man," and "Between the Wars" (U.S. diplomatic history from Versailles to Pearl Harbor, narrated by Eric Sevareid).

Future Relationships Between Business and the Press

It is ironic that for the purpose of a discussion such as this, two categories have to be established — "business" on the one hand, and "media" or the "press" on the other. The irony lies in the obvious fact that the "press" is itself a business, with the need to earn a profit or go under. The alternative is a government press, and neither "business" nor the "press" wants to see the government become the purveyor of the nation's news.

So it becomes urgent that both business and the media heal the breach between them and find ways to achieve certain common goals in the public interest. The role of the press, after all, should be to provide a forum so that the American people can be fully informed and thereby make intelligent decisions. The business community has both the right and obligation to participate in that forum.

If there is any one marketplace in America that must remain totally free and open, it is the marketplace of ideas. With the free and open flow of news and opinion as the overriding objective, business and the press alike must strive toward the following sub-objectives:

1. Recognition that in a pluralistic society, an unfettered flow of information is in the public interest.

2. The public should be exposed to a diversity of information and a diversity of viewpoints, from as many political, social, and economic sectors as possible.

3. De facto censorship — the erection of artificial barriers to the public print and airwaves alike — should be as reprehensible as censorship of the news by the government.

The achievement of these objectives will require major effort by business and media. Here are some suggestions for those in the news business:

1. Television, particularly the networks, must recognize that an access problem exists, and then move to correct it. If a newspaper story distorts or ignores a point of view, remedies are available. Newspapers print letters to the editor. They accept advocacy advertisements. Some papers — notably the *Washington Post* — have appointed ombudsmen to serve as inspectors general who police the papers themselves. Television networks do none of these things. And they should. Needed is the right to reply, to set the record straight — on prime time, if the attack or sin of omission was made in prime time. Ideally, this right to respond or comment should be free; as a last resort, commercial time should be made available, even if it means some adjustment of the equal time doctrine.

2. More newspapers need to develop the op-ed page concept; a regular place in the newspaper where all shades of opinion may be heard, and where essays should be invited from as disparate a group as possible. Although newspapers publish letters to the editor, the letters page has obvious shortcomings. Letters, by necessity, must be kept as short as possible. They

usually appear in response to something already published, generally after considerable time has elapsed. This time lag often dilutes the effectiveness of the response. The op-ed page, on the other hand, provides a timelier, more thoughtful forum.

3. Journalists in all the media must strive to improve their professional skills and standards. Fairness and objectivity should be nurtured, and sensationalism recognized and rooted out. They must remember selection is censorship. Print journalists know when they haven't contacted all the parties in a dispute. News editors know when they've reported an indictment on page one, and ignored the dismissal. TV anchor people know when they've selected a 30-second snippet from an interview that took two hours to tape. They must constantly fight the temptation to sell a few extra papers or gain a fraction of a rating point at the expense of their professionalism.

4. News executives of every stripe must recognize that complex issues require informed handling, and that "instant experts" aren't experts at all. People who cover business news must be well educated and well trained. And, because of the complexities of industries like energy, many business reporters must be trained as specialists. Would any sports editor send his tennis expert to cover the Super Bowl? Aren't jobs, the economy, trade deficits, currency fluctuations, and energy as important as sports?

Business, for its part, also has some homework to do:

1. Businessmen must make themselves available to the press, even if some of them have been burned in the past. At Mobil, we conduct a regular program of media lunches, at which newspeople meet our top executives, with what's said "on the record." Our experience has been that most journalists honestly want to learn about our business, and we've also found that many of our own people had little prior knowledge about some of the pressures newspeople labor under.

2. The "no comment" syndrome should be avoided. Unless the businessman knows for a fact that the questioner means to embarrass him, or has an atrocious track record, it's far better to say "I don't know, but I'll try to find out and call you back." And then the promised call must be made. If business and the media are to heal their breach, mutual trust must be established, albeit at the risk of some pain.

3. Business must be prepared to engage in dialogue. This means going beyond the suggestions made in points one and two, if necessary. A business that has been candid with the press,

and has attempted to communicate, may still find itself ignored, or its position distorted. In that case, the advertising option should be considered. As already indicated, business has not only the right but the *obligation* to speak out and participate in the forum of ideas.

4. Business also has the obligation to educate — to reach the schools and universities either through grants or through the participation of its executives in programs that teach such things as basic economics. Journalists, after all, come to their craft from the campus, and the more they learn about how our economic system works in school, the less they'll have to learn on the job. The marketplace of ideas is much broader than today's newspaper or the six o'clock news, and business has a role to play at many levels.

The reconciliation of the press and business probably will be an evolutionary process, rather than a revolutionary one, and there is evidence that the print media and business are already well along in the process. Television, unfortunately, still has a lot of catching up to do. And the time to start is now.

Ideals in Collision: The Relationship between Business and the News Media

Leonard Silk
The New York Times

I am not sure who is on trial today — business, the news media, or both. If I were forced to answer, on pain of possible indictment for perjury, I would have to say it is the media who are here as the defendants, this being the annual Benjamin F. Fairless Memorial Lectures, normally the occasion for high-level corporate statesmanship and public suffering over the problems that have beset the free-enterprise system, one of which is regarded in board rooms all over America as "the media."

I should like to make clear from the outset, however, that I do not consider my role today to serve as defense attorney for the media. I am a newspaperman and an economist, but not a lawyer. My aim — which comes out of my own professional background — is to be objective, fair, and disinterested; that is, not to be a pleader for the special interests of either business or the media. Incidentally, I speak today only for myself, not for *The New York Times* nor other news media.

I confess that I have a good deal of trouble with that word, "media," partly because it was originally a Madison Avenue expression which regards newspapers, magazines, radio and television essentially as intermediaries for advertising and publicity between corporations and their customers, and partly because I associate "the media" (especially when used in the singular) with the pejorative use to which the term was put by former Vice President Spiro Agnew before his fall from grace and power. Businessmen often complain that to much of the public, profit has become a dirty word. I am afraid that to many businessmen, "the media" has become a dirty word.

So I hope that you will forgive me if I prefer to use the term "the press" rather than "the media" to denominate an institution deemed by our Founding Fathers as worthy of special respect and protection in the Constitution, even though I realize that some of the most influential journalism today is electronic. Someday all journalism may be electronic, at least in the sense that there will be no technology remaining that involves the physical pressure of sculpted type upon a sheet of paper.

But, even if the printing press should vanish altogether someday (and the pressmen with it), I fervently hope that "the press" will survive in all its Areopagitical and Constitutional splendor. For a free press will always remain as vital to a free society as in the days of John Milton or Thomas Jefferson. There may be no such thing as a free lunch or free media, but there *is* such a thing as a free press. There is also such a thing as a kept press, a timid press, and an ineffectual press — and most countries in the world have all three. It would be no blessing for the United States of America to follow their example. The danger of having a free, vigorous, and honest press transformed into a kept, timid, and ineffectual press stems not just from government or outside business pressures, but from within the media — when the commercial objectives of publishers and stockholders undermine or subvert news and editorial values.

The Ideals of the Press

Our discussion has been entitled "Ideals in Collision," and it might be well for me to start by considering the ideals of the press. One of those key ideals, as I have already suggested, is to be *disinterested* — that is, to pursue the truth no matter whose interest is affected and how. It is an ideal that honest reporters and editors share with the best publishers.

Adolph S. Ochs expressed that ideal in words that are hallowed and immortal, certainly to us at *The New York Times*: "To give the news, without fear or favor, regardless of any party, sect or interest involved." That principle was published on the editorial page of *The Times* on August 19, 1896, when Mr. Ochs assumed responsibility for the paper. Interestingly enough, it ran under the heading "Business Announcement." Disinterest was properly regarded as vital to the business of the newspaper, and of the public.

Some publishers have put their credos in more crusading terms. Thus, on April 10, 1907, on the occasion of his "retirement" as publisher of *The St. Louis Post-Dispatch* and *The New York World* — a retirement that proved to be premature and inoperative — Joseph Pulitzer declared his faith that his newspapers would continue to adhere to certain "cardinal principles" which he stated as ". . . always fight for progress and reform, never tolerate injustice or corruption, always fight demagogues of all parties, never belong to any party, always oppose privileged classes and public plunderers, never lack sympathy with the poor, always remain devoted to the public welfare, never be satisfied with merely printing news, always be drastically independent, never be afraid to attack wrong, whether by predatory plutocracy or predatory poverty."

Whether expressed in the flaming rhetoric of a Pulitzer or the somber tones of an Ochs, the traditional claim of the outstanding American publisher is that he is responsive and responsible to the public interest. It is that service to the public interest that merits the special protection accorded to freedom of speech and freedom of the press in the First Amendment of the Constitution.

Obviously those rights do not belong to the press alone but to all citizens. The question "Who elected the press?" is, in my view, as silly as asking who elected the citizen to voice his views on public issues; these are inalienable rights in a free society. Press freedom does not require neutrality or sterility on controversial issues; the opposite is true. Indeed, press freedom does not even *require* responsibility on the part of the press, although I believe that publishers and editors and reporters should voluntarily assume it. As a later *Times* publisher, Arthur Hays Sulzberger, said in 1947, "As a newspaper we live under certain guarantees of freedom, and it is important to point out that there is no quid pro quo written into the Constitution. Freedom is granted — responsibility is not required." He added that freedom of the press implies the right to be biased. A sectarian newspaper is naturally biased in favor of the particular faith that it serves,and should be protected in its right to be so prejudiced; and so should Mobil Oil or any other business. But a newspaper of general circulation, as Mr. Sulzberger said, does have the obligation to inform its readers "on all sides of every important issue." The only question is how that obligation is to be interpreted, and by whom, and how it is to be enforced. I hold that the obligation is one that cannot be imposed by the State, or press freedom has no meaning, nor by any other outside force; the sense of obligation or responsibility to the broad public must be voluntary on the part of the press, and control must be internal.

Various news media discharge this responsibility better or worse, never perfectly; I have no idea what the word "perfectly" in this context would mean. The press in a capitalistic nation is inherently a schizoid institution. The split or tension within a given newspaper or television network is that while it asserts its dedication to the public interest, it also pursues its financial self-interest. For that reason, the best news media have always sought to enforce a strict separation between their editorial and business sides, while the worst allowed the business side to dominate and control the news and editorial function. This is very different from other commercial businesses. Can you imagine a manufacturing company, or oil company, or bank, that allowed its public relations department or advertising agency or press section or house organ to be independent of its business managers? But in an honest newspaper this must be so. And I am concerned that, with the growth of newspaper chains and the electronic media into big business, the balance within too much of the American press has been tilting toward the business side. The proprietors of the news media nowadays bow to no other business executives in asserting their devotion to the "bottom line"; this is the reason why many observers, including Chief Justice Burger of the United States Supreme Court, assert that they can see no difference between so-called "media conglomerates" and other business corporations.

Indeed, as a business operation, the media are as accountable as any other business — accountable to the S.E.C., to the I.R.S., and to all other governmental regulatory agencies; and the press is as subject to all laws, including the libel laws, as any other business or individual. It is only the *press* function — freedom of the press from government control — that is specially protected, and that is a function or a right that is protected for all citizens, including corporate managers.

Freedom of the press includes the right not to publish as well as to publish. Should newspaper publishers not have the right to protect their readers from unscrupulous advertisers? Should they not have the right to exercise their taste — the right not to serve an audience hungry for pornography? Should they not have the right to exercise their news and editorial judgment? Would Mobil Oil or any other corporation be willing to accord equal time in company pronouncements or equal space in company advertising, including advocacy advertising, to Ralph Nader — or all the other groups that are critical of, or disagree with the accuracy of the facts presented by a corporation? Should stockholders be compelled, by law, to be exposed to all shades

43

of opinion, with equal time, on all the issues that come before them? And, if not, why should any given newspaper or television station be compelled to publish or air whatever anyone wishes it to disseminate on any or every issue?

I see no contradiction here with what I said before: the obligation of a newspaper of general circulation such as *The Times* to inform its readers on all sides of every important issue. This is what we have sought to do, and have sought to do better, by creating the op ed page for dissenting opinions (this was done almost nine years ago, and the example has been followed widely), and by expanding our letters column, by printing daily corrections of errors, by trying to be both fair and accurate, recognizing that pure truth is awfully hard to come by, and that subjective views of an event or a fact or an issue often differ. But in the end there is only so much space or air time, and editors must decide how best to use that space or time. Who else can or should make that decision? Government officials? Business executives? Labor leaders? For anyone who genuinely believes in a free press, the question answers itself. Which is not to say that the judgment and decisions of editors cannot be questioned or criticized; they can be, should be, and they are. There is nothing that we do in the dark — at least nothing that we do that does not see the light of day the next day. We live in a gold fish bowl and we can be punished (or destroyed) in many ways, including by a loss of circulation and advertising, if readers or advertisers dislike what they see.

Television stations face even more instantaneous financial punishment when they make the wrong decisions about what to put on the air. I believe that is the main reason they are so resistant to accepting advocacy advertising from corporations. It is the fear of dial-switching, as listeners tune out an explanation of the economics of gas pricing or energy development for a rock singer, a baseball game, a quiz show, a soap opera, or some other piece of entertainment that will raise its ratings and hence its advertising dollars and profits. That is the same reason why news itself and the arts and sciences and social sciences, including economics, get so little air time on commercial channels; thank goodness some corporations, including Mobil, do so much to make room for news analysis and the arts on public television.

Yet I do believe that television stations should modify their practices, and curb their profit-making appetites, enough to make room for more advocacy advertising and responses — as well as for more news, news analysis, and coverage of the arts and sciences. Whether I actually expect them to rush to do so, now that they have heard the word, is another matter; given profit objectives and the intensity of competition in the ratings game, I would be astonished if they did. But the corporations have every right to press for more coverage, more freedom to express and air their views, and for greater accuracy. That obviously holds for newspapers and other print media as well as for television.

Readers, including corporate executives, do both us and the public a service by such criticism, by forcing us to achieve higher standards of accuracy and fairness. Mobil in particular has done a service in bringing public issues of great concern to it to the fore; it has helped to stimulate robust and open debate, especially through its op ed page ads. We are wrong if we are any more sensitive or resentful of criticism or the discovery of error than the corporations, government, or any other group whom we cover or deign to criticize.

But I do think there is a question of scale and degree concerning advocacy advertising. It may be that Mobil alone cannot be charged with dominating public discussion when, as the company's vice president of public affairs, Herbert Schmertz, told a House subcommittee on May 25, 1978, Mobil spent only $3.2 million on "non-deductible" advertising in 1977 — non-deductible because it was judged by Mobil and its lawyers to possess political content. Mr. Schmertz said his chief concern was not with the tax aspect itself but with "the chilling effect that unequal enforcement of the tax rules and signaling out various business groups for special scrutiny has on the public's right to information from all sources." But what if all the Fortune 500 corporations spent only what Mobil did on political or advocacy advertising; the sum would come to $1.6 billion. What other group or groups could begin to match that? And what if Mr. Schmertz were right and the "chilling effect" of tax scrutiny were removed, what then would be the volume of corporate advocacy advertising? Since total advertising outlays in 1977 came to about $37 billion, the potential for a blanketing out of other groups' expressions of opinion on political or environmental or social issues is surely there.

Mr. Schmertz does raise an interesting point in asking why "media conglomerates" can freely editorialize on political issues, without treating those editorials as non-deductible, where nonmedia corporations cannot. It is not, I take it, that Mr.

Schmertz or Mobil wishes to contract the rights of the press but rather to expand the rights of other business corporations. More broadly, the issue may be stated as follows: Should the press be entitled to any privilege or protection not accorded to all business corporations? Conversely, should not all business corporations have the same First Amendment rights possessed by the press — that is, by "media conglomerates?"

The Bellotti Decision

The United States Supreme Court has recently been exploring those issues. On April 26, 1978, the Supreme Court struck down a Massachusetts law that had limited the First Amendment rights of a business corporation to those issues "that materially affect its business, property or assets." By a 5-to-4 decision, the court held, in *First National Bank of Boston et al v. Bellotti*, that the appellants — national banking associations and business corporations — had the right to spend corporate funds to publicize their views opposing a referendum to authorize the Massachusetts legislature to enact a graduated personal income tax.

Does this decision mean, as some hope and others fear, that a corporation — an "artificial being, invisible, intangible, and existing only in contemplation of law," as Chief Justice John Marshall defined it in the Dartmouth case of 1819 — has now acquired the same political rights as a natural person?

In *Bellotti*, the Supreme Court did not go nearly that far. Even in the area of free speech, the court did not affirm the identity of individual and corporate rights. Writing for the majority, Justice Lewis F. Powell, Jr. stated that the Superior Court of Massachusetts, in framing the key question as whether and to what extent corporations have First Amendment rights, had posed the wrong question. The proper question, Justice Powell said, is not whether corporations "have" First Amendment rights and, if so, whether they are coextensive with those of natural persons, but rather whether the Massachusetts law abridged expressions of views that the First Amendment was meant to protect for the sake of the broad society. "We hold it does," said Mr. Powell, speaking for the majority.

But, in rejecting the finding of the Massachusetts Superior Court that corporate speech is protected only when it pertains directly to the corporation's business interests, Justice Powell specifically said, "We need not survey the outer boundaries of the amendment's protection of corporate speech, nor address the abstract question whether corporations have the full measure of rights that individuals enjoy under the First Amendment." Simply put, he added, the key question was "whether the corporate identity of the speaker deprives this proposed speech of what otherwise would be its clear entitlement to protection." And he cited a 1945 Supreme Court decision in *Thomas v. Collins* in justifying the majority's verdict in the *Bellotti* case to overrule "a restriction so destructive of the right of public discussion, without greater or more imminent danger to the public interest than existed in this case."

In some other case involving greater and more clearly demonstrated public danger, the majority of the court might have ruled — and might still rule — the other way. In response to the arguments made by the Massachusetts Attorney General that "corporations are wealthy and powerful and their views may drown out other points of view," Justice Powell said that if such arguments were supported "by record of legislative findings that corporate advocacy threatened imminently to undermine democratic processes, thereby denigrating rather than serving First Amendment interests, these arguments would merit our consideration."

The very narrowness of the 5-to-4 decision should warn the managers of corporations not to assume some sort of clear breakthrough in establishing their rights to use corporate assets ("stockholders' money") to campaign for political causes. Justice William H. Rehnquist, a Nixon appointee who is generally considered one of the more conservative members of the court, agreeing with the dissenting minority in *Bellotti*, declared: "A state grants to a business corporation the blessings of a potentially perpetual life and limited liability to enhance its efficiency as an economic entity. It might reasonably be concluded that those properties, so beneficial in the economic sphere, pose special dangers in the political sphere." That is a view that many conservatives and liberals share, and a small shift in the composition of the court could shift the balance toward stricter limits on the political powers of corporations.

Bellotti was no Magna Carta for business corporations. Corporations are still barred from giving financial support to politicians or candidates for political office, and the broad question left unanswered is how independent or sterile a corporation's activities must be when it speaks out on a public issue or supports particular candidates or parties. Corporations taking stands on political issues must proceed carefully lest they violate the Federal Corrupt Practices Act or other Federal and state laws restricting corporate political activity.

Business would be well advised to avoid rekindling public distrust, which reached a low point in 1973-76. The fall of business in public esteem, registered in poll after poll, was significantly due to the public reaction to Watergate and to corrupt practices of some businesses at home and abroad. Business, having been badly burned, should in my view proceed with great caution in its political activities, lest the public decide that corporations are using their wealth and power to dominate the political process. The force of public opinion in influencing legislative and regulatory curbs on business should never be underestimated, and if business hopes to avoid a resurgence of damaging regulations, it must avoid antagonizing public opinion.

The same counsel applies to the press. In a democratic society, every institution, whether business or the press, is endangered if it loses public support and "consent."

Media Conglomerates and The Quest for Profits

Is there any more reason to worry about the power of banks, oil companies, manufacturers or other nonmedia corporations to achieve an unfair advantage over groups or individuals and dominate the political process than about the power of the "media conglomerates?" Chief Justice Burger has, in fact, contended that the publishing conglomerates "pose a much more realistic threat to valid interests" than do "corporations not regularly concerned with shaping public opinion on public issues." He has stressed "the difficulty, and perhaps impossibility, of distinguishing, either as a matter of fact or constitutional law," media corporations from other business corporations, and has said that he perceives no basis for saying that the managers and directors of media conglomerates are more or less sensitive to the views and desires of minority shareholders than corporate officers generally. "Nor can it be said," he added, "even if relevant to First Amendment analysis — which it is not — that the former are more virtuous, wise or restrained in the exercise of corporate power than the latter." Skepticism and even cynicism about the distinterestedness and social responsibility of the press — not only of journalists but of "the managers and directors of media conglomerates" in Chief Justice Burger's language — is widespread nowadays.

Many business executives blame the press for their own drop in public esteem. They accuse the press of seizing upon and exaggerating business scandals or questionable acts in a way that smears all business. Many executives feel that the press, far from educating the public on how the free-enterprise system works to serve individual and social needs, undermines support for the system. In effect, they charge the press with hypocrisy for professing high ideals while practicing distortion and untruth for the sake of "selling papers" and making money.

This criticism, coming from businessmen, would seem to conflict with traditional business ideology: If the free-enterprise system is so effective in serving consumer and public interests, and if profit is the best guide to resource allocation and the just reward for serving the public, then what is wrong with a publisher's trying to sell more papers and advertising, or a broadcaster's trying to boost a network's ratings by giving the public "what it wants?"

But those businessmen who sense that there is something wrong when the press puts its own financial interests above the broad public interest are right; they recognize that the press does have responsibility to the public, and to truth, which must take precedence over its immediate quest for profit. Some businessmen would say that the same applies to any other business, and it is not possible to draw a sharp line between the press and other businesses. Yet there is a significant difference in the degree to which the press is expected to be a public-interest institution and other businesses are properly regarded as limited-purpose organizations which often deceive themselves when they try to portray their special interests as identical with the public interest. Every corporate official is tempted to commit the mistake made by "Engine Charley" Wilson of General Motors when he declared, "What is good for the country is good for General Motors, and vice versa." It ain't necessarily so. But the mistake, if it is not regarded as hypocritical or deliberately deceptive, is readily forgiven by the public. Nobody really expects General Motors or Mobil to serve as the voice of the people.

But the press is held to different standards. It is considered outrageous, and properly so, when a newspaper lets its own quest for profits dictate its editors' judgment of the news, how to play it, what to cover, what not to cover, and how to editorialize about it or stand silent. An honest, accurate, disinterested, and courageous press is what economists call a "public good" — something from which the entire community stands to benefit. However, the payments for the benefits resulting from that public good may not go to those who create it. In fact, a good newspaper may die, though it served its community well — as did, for instance, *The New York Herald-Tribune,* which we at *The Times* still miss, or *The Chicago Daily News,* which Chicago ought to miss, if it has enough sense, because it served Chicago well, if not its own financial interests.

As business wants the understanding and, where merited, the support of the press (as an aside, may I say that it is a tribute to the importance of a free and disinterested press that business wants its good opinion so much), so the press would like better comprehension from business of its own role, even when it clashes with the interests of a particular company or industry. An open and highly decentralized political and economic system needs a free, intelligent and honest press, if it is to survive. The press helps to bind a loose and pluralistic society together; even the President's Cabinet lives off its daily information and measures itself by its perceptions and judgments. The press is equally important for business and other elements in a free society. But business, which knows how to value freedom and autonomy for itself, sometimes seems to care less about the freedom of the press from government or judicial restraint, or about the effect of business pressures in deadening press freedom, where particular companies or industries are able to exert such pressures against a particular publication, or against the press generally.

Corporations and Public Issues

In what ways, then, should corporations seek to influence social values and political decisions? Individual corporations are bound to differ in their judgment as to the best answer to that question. Some will choose to play a conspicuous and aggressive role in fighting against positions advanced by other interest groups or politicians or newspapers or individual authors with whom they disagree. As some are already doing, more corporations will mount campaigns through institutional advertising in the press, and eventually, it seems possible to me, on television. Many companies have already taken advantage of the Federal Election Campaign Act Amendments of 1976 to form Political Action Committees, using contributed funds from stockholders to support candidates who support policies and legislation favored by the corporations, and others will follow suit.

Many corporations, however, are likely to choose to play a

more restrained and less conspicuous or assertive role on public issues, concluding — often on the basis of survey evidence — that too aggressive and strident an attack by corporations on those with whom they disagree is likely to be counterproductive by antagonizing much of the public, especially opinion leaders.

The largest and most powerful companies are often likely to be the ones most sensitive to the danger of provoking a hostile reaction by seeming to throw their weight around. In some cases, corporate officials are likely to decide that the political process serves the interests of the business community best when it wins the confidence of diverse interest groups, and that business is wisest not to shatter confidence in the democratic process. Business could deepen cynicism and distrust of public officials and politicans by using its influence in what may be perceived as a gross and self-serving way.

This will hold for business's relations not only with the press but with other institutions, such as research centers, public foundations, and our colleges and universities. I think, to take a specific case, that Mobil made a serious mistake in withdrawing its financial support from the Bagehot Fellows program at Columbia University, a program designed to improve the professional qualifications of economic journalists, because Mobil disapproved of the choice of a new man to head the program. Fortunately several other companies, including one major oil company, continued or increased their support for the Bagehot program, and it has survived. But I believe that damage has been done to Mobil itself.

There are many hostile and angry voices within the business community today, and in my view they are helping to raise the noise level and making it harder to resolve important national issues reasonably and rationally. I know that business feels set upon, but it should not overreact. If society is polarized, business itself will suffer. Threat begets counterthreat, vituperation begets countervituperation, and hostility escalates.

Business does have a great deal to contribute to public debates on many issues and to the political process, and it has every right to safeguard and try to advance its own interests. The public — all of us, including other parts of the business community itself, which is highly diverse and often in conflict within itself — has every reason to listen to what individual corporations know and say and want, as part of the process of reaching major policy decisions.

Hence, every business not only has the right but even the obligation to provide the public with information, analyses, and its own best judgments as a means of helping to strengthen the policy-making process. I believe that business will be most effective if it does not, however strongly it may feel about particular issues, try to smother the democratic process or use its financial weight or political influence to dominate or silence other voices in the community, in the academic world, or in the press. As Robert Wiebe said of American business in its relationship to the progressive movement during the first two decades of this century, "Where businessmen adopted a conciliatory approach, they maximized their chances of success."[1]

Today, as in the past, in arriving at its public policy positions, business needs to listen to what other groups or individuals are saying, to be sure that it has addressed the real public interests and concerns. All the best minds are not on corporate payrolls, nor need everyone else share a business ideology to have something valuable to contribute to society.

Corporations choosing to intervene on public issues should themselves invest sufficient time and intellectual resources to assure themselves that they have seen particular issues in all their dimensions and are not vulnerable to the charge of being merely ideological or narrowly self-interested. Pursuit of one's own interest is accepted by the American public as both inevitable and proper (certainly as legitimate) but piety and false patriotism it can do without.

Business leaders should seek to engage in face-to-face dialogue with interested groups and individuals, not simply depend on their own (or their intellectual advisers') partisan interpretation of the inner thinking or public statements of other groups. If more information helps the public, it also will help business. Businessmen, for some reason, have trouble in recognizing that communication is a two-way street, or rather that it is a great city with many streets and avenues and alleys and ghettoes. A free and responsible press should help business and the rest of society by exploring them all.

When corporate management arrives at a position on a public issue, it should present its view in a fair and open way, providing as much supporting evidence for its view as it can. If business argues reasonably and fairly for what it believes, it will avoid provoking public antagonism.

Management should avoid deciding prematurely that there is one and only one right answer to every public issue. Public issues are usually complex, involving conflicts among several objectives which may involve trade-offs or compromises to reach workable solutions. Admittedly, these may sometimes be second-best or third-best solutions, but in an imperfect world — and a democratic society — these may be better than no solutions at all.

I feel strongly that our society urgently requires increased cooperation between business and government, and between business and other groups in the community. This will be essential if the nation is to solve persistent problems of economic growth and stability, eliminate high unemployment and inflation, reduce the social and international tensions that result from inequality and poverty, arrest urban decay, avert threats to the natural environment and build a healthy social order in which both business and governmental institutions can regain high public regard. The stability and future development of our society depend on it.

Businessmen, in my experience, have been seriously shaken by their fall in public regard in recent years and are eager to reverse that trend. There is no simple formula for how business can regain public respect and understanding, and play a more constructive role in public debates, since what is involved is everything that individual executives and corporations do in the conduct of their business and in their relations with government and the public, at home and abroad. What corporate executives need to accept is that they have not one but two major roles to play — one in managing the internal affairs of their companies and doing so profitably, and the other in recognizing and responding intelligently to the expectations and needs of the broad society. If they neglect the second role, they are likely to get themselves and their organizations in trouble and public disrepute, as some have already done.

The Power of the Media

The press has certainly played an active role in exposing such scandals: and many businessmen, while deploring wrongdoing, still blame the press for overplaying stories of business corruption and damaging the reputation of all business. Business believes that the press has the power to shape public opinion, for good or evil, but uses that power to undermine those in authority, promote dissension and public turmoil, and seize upon the poor behavior of a few businesses as a way of advancing an anti-business ideology. As some businessmen see it, "Even though the press is a business, it doesn't reflect business values." And many share the view that "unless the press stops tearing down our system and begins to tell the public how it works, business leaders will not be permitted any future participation in the formation of social goals."

Most journalists and publishers are at a loss to know how to respond to such charges. I should like to assure you that my own lifetime of experience leads me to the conclusion that the vast majority of journalists do not regard themselves as subversive, do not think they are trying to undermine the system, and want to live within the system. They want their community and its businesses — including their own paper — to prosper. They feel that they are trying to do a professional and honest job, and that a free press worthy of the name is bound to be a critical press; they consider such a press to be a strength, not a weakness, of a free and healthy society. No group (including both business and the press itself) likes to be criticized or have its faults exposed; but a courageous press is one that is prepared to do that job, for the sake of the broad public interest.

It is no easy job to discover and expose unpleasant or unwelcome truths about powerful elements in our society — whether these are particular corporations where officials have engaged in wrongdoing, or the military, the C.I.A., the F.B.I., or even the presidency of the United States. Paradoxically, it has been the exposure of wrongdoing in high places that has been the source of deep public and business concern about the press, and not only because the messenger is blamed for the message. For, even though the press proved to be *right* about the major political and business scandals it covered, the press disclosed itself to be *powerful*, and power is feared and often hated.

As Professor Samuel P. Huntington of Harvard — now a White House aide — has written,

> In the two most dramatic domestic policy conflicts of the Nixon administration — the Pentagon Papers and Watergate — organs of the national media challenged and defeated the national executive. The press, indeed, played a leading role in bringing about what no other single institution, group, or combination of institutions and groups had done previously in American history: forcing out of office a president who had been elected less than two years earlier by one of the largest popular majorities in American history. No future president can or will forget that fact.[2]

Professor Huntington contends that the most notable new

source of national power to emerge in recent years has been the national media, by which he means "the national TV networks, the national news magazines, and the major newspapers with national reach such as the *Washington Post* and *The New York Times.*"

The possession of power in democratic societies breeds anxiety about the misuse of power and evokes demands that power be curbed; this is as true for the press as it is for the large corporation — or for government itself. Where the press is concerned, this anxiety sometimes takes the form of asking: "Who elected the press? Who gives the press the right to speak for us? Do they really represent us? What are their true motives?" There is a streak of populism and perhaps anti-intellectualism in those questions.

But, contradictorily, at other times the demand is that "the responsibility of the press should now be increased to be commensurate with its power; significant measures are required to restore an appropriate balance between the press, the government, and other institutions in society," as the Trilateral Commission put it. This represents not a populist but an elitist, establishmentarian view of what should be done to increase the "governability" of a democracy. According to this view, advanced by the Trilateral Commission, the press, like the business corporation, must behave with "social responsibility" now that it has achieved great national power; but, it is asserted, the press has been stubbornly resisting such social responsibility just as the corporations once did:

> . . . The increase in media power is not unlike the rise of the industrial corporation to national power at the end of the nineteenth century. Just as the corporations enveloped themselves in the constitutional protection of the due process clause, the media now defend themselves in terms of the First Amendment. In both cases, there obviously are important rights to be protected, but broader interests of society and government are also at stake. In due course, beginning with the Interstate Commerce Act and the Sherman Antitrust Act, measures had to be taken to regulate the new industrial centers of power and to define their relations to the rest of society. Something comparable appears to be now needed with respect to the media. [3]

Such talk is anathema to proprietors of the news media. The First Amendment rights to free speech and a free press (which are not the possession of the "institutional press" alone) are not to be treated as comparable to property rights and the freedom to pursue commercial interests. They belong to all citizens.

Yet is is true that freedom and power may conflict. The issue that the news media cannot avoid is that of their own *power*. And if it is necessary, as I believe it is, to worry about the potential danger of dominance by large business corporations over the political process, then it is also necessary to worry, as Chief Justice Burger obviously does, about the dominance of media conglomerates.

The problem of "media power" will not disappear. It is more likely to keep on growing, jeopardizing the ability of minority or dissenting voices to be heard, and endangering the professionalism of those who work as reporters and editors or newscasters. To me, this implies that those who work as newsmen and seek to develop truthful reports and analyses of important public matters must not be merely the agents of powerful executives but have the freedom to do their job as conscientious, honest, competent professionals, serving the public interest and, as one puts it on the witness stand, telling the truth, the whole truth, and nothing but the truth.

This is the most important ideal of the journalist, the editor, the writer. It is what drew the best of us to this peculiar and difficult calling. It is why we love it, when we do, and why we try to stay in it, if we can. The ideal of independence and integrity for journalists should, I strongly believe, be safeguarded for the sake of the society — just as the academic freedom of professors is safeguarded from administrative or external political control, or the independence and integrity of judges is protected from those who wield public or private power.

The ideal of professional integrity may on occasion bring the journalist into conflict with his own publisher or the publisher's chosen deputies. Those who want to preserve and strengthen a free society will, I hope, therefore want to safeguard the freedom of journalists to do their job without fear or favor to any interest, internal or external.

High professional standards and diversity of views are, in my opinion, the essential requirement for a truly free national press — one that will deserve and, I believe, gain the confidence, respect, and support of every major element in our society, including business, which knows how to appreciate quality and integrity.

Business should recognize that a free press, dedicated to the public interest, fundamentally helps to create the kind of society in which free economic as well as political institutions can survive and prosper.

But, if it is to gain such recognition, the press has the corresponding obligation and responsibility to be fair, to be balanced, to be competent, and to be honestly critical in its treatment of government, business, labor, and all other groups, including the press itself.

(1) R.H. Wiebe, *Businessmen and Reform: A Study of the Progressive Movement* (Cambridge: Harvard University Press, 1962), p. 215.

(2) *The Crisis of Democracy,* Report on the Governability of Democracies to the Trilateral Commission. (New York: New York University Press, 1977), pp. 99-100.

(3)Ibid., pp. 181-182.

Following the lectures each speaker was invited to respond to the other's presentation.

Response by Mr. Warner:

I am not going to take long, because in many respects I find myself in agreement with Leonard. I hope it came through in my prepared remarks that we at Mobil have a very high regard for *The New York Times*. We can have honest and hard differences of opinion but there is no paper like *The Times*.

I have, Leonard, a bit of understanding about the schizoid character of a free press. I do understand the absolute need for the editorial staff not to be impinged upon by the business side. Believe me, if you carry away one thing with you today, it is my very strong conviction that the only thing we can have is a free press; if we lose that we will have lost a very, very great deal. And I hope you don't believe that we in Mobil are suggesting anything but a free press.

With regard to television, I realize the networks don't want to allow advocacy advertising because they don't know where to stop it and they don't know how to stop it. If they give Mobil an opportunity to express its views, they don't know whether four others will want the same opportunity. And if they have to make the time free, what happens to their bottom line? I have told some of the heads of those networks that I think the T.V. networks are heading into trouble unless they find a mechanism for allowing the other voices to be heard. If they don't they will end up with three or four people deciding what goes on television — and that gets awfully arrogant and awfully difficult to accept. I would much prefer to see the networks handle the problem themselves rather than to have government ultimately get into it, because I know that won't work.

I agree with you, Leonard, the *Bellotti* decision that I quoted is a narrow decision. Any time the Supreme Court comes down with a 5-4 decision, it's a narrow decision. It was also narrow in another respect. Justice Powell went out of his way to be certain that the decision did not impinge on the Federal Corrupt Practices Act. In that respect it was quite narrowing.

Finally, I think you built a strawman when you expressed a fear that every corporation might start advocacy advertising. We have had advocacy advertising for eight years and have been totally unsuccessful in getting more than one or two companies to follow our example. My instinct is that in this kind of thing each company is going to do its own thing, and will not necessarily follow what we are doing. So be it.

I'm proud of what we are doing. I'm proud that we are having what I think is a reasonable impact.

Response by Mr. Silk:

I, too, appreciate everything that Rawleigh says. In the interest of accuracy, I must say that he is right on the strawman remarks. I was using a kind of *reductio* position to say what it would be like if everybody would do the same thing.

It is extremely interesting to see why everyone does not do the same thing. Even within the oil industry I have spoken with some people who don't believe that what Mobil is doing makes sense in terms of Mobil's relations with the public or government. I think some people feel that business incurs antagonisms when it seems to throw its weight around and that it would be better for business to try to adopt in its public statements a more modest or conciliatory stance.

That position deserves respect. It is not necessarily founded on timidity. There is a tendency nowadays for people who feel differently to pound the table and say "You are all a group of 'ninnies' because you don't have the guts to speak up!" To some extent the hesitancy of some large corporations to push advocacy advertising may be the instinctive feeling that because they do have a lot of money and a lot of power they will get along better in the society if they are somewhat less conspicious in deploying that money and power.

The question of how one addresses this issue is vital. Mobil's ads are brisk, robust, by-and-large accurate, and carefully researched. I wish I could say the same thing for all advocacy advertising, much of which is simplistic, exaggerated, and demagogic.

I agree with all of Rawleigh's conclusions. The only one I want to comment on is the need for increased professionalism in the press. I believe that the first requirement of professionalism is to be independent of your clients — which also means being independent of your employer. A doctor who works for a mining company, for example, would certainly violate his Hippocratic oath if he asserted that miners with black lung or brown lung did not really have such a condition. In the same way, an engineer who says an airplane is ready to fly when he knows it is not ready to fly would be guilty of criminal misconduct. Whatever professionalism is, it describes a community of fellow professionals who have standards that must be met.

Being an editor may not look as if it is a profession, but it is. Let me quote a news item from *The New York Times*:

> Lansing, Mich. — June 25. John P. McGoff, who heads companies that publish eight daily newspapers and more than 40 weeklies in several states, has discharged two of his Michigan editors after they failed to obey orders to run provocative articles that were highly critical of President Carter.
>
> One of the articles said that the President condoned promiscuity among members of his staff. The other suggested he was grooming his wife, Rosalyn, to be a future vice president.
>
> They were written by George Bernard, the newly-hired bureau chief for Mr. McGoff's Panax newspaper chain, and were distributed to his newspapers two weeks ago along with a front-office memorandum labeling them explosive and urging that they be given front-page display . . .

The two men who were fired had won journalism awards in the State and were well-respected in Michigan press circles. Their conduct is an example of what I mean by professionalism. This disregard of professionalism is something that could endanger our country. We cannot have that kind of a press.

Question and Answer Period

Question for Mr. Silk:

What is the difference, if any, between a newspaper expressing its opinions and biases through an editorial and a corporation doing the same through paid advertising?

That is a tough question but my answer — and I have thought about this quite a lot — is that it *is* a newspaper's business to publish news and editorialize about it. A non-media corporation is chartered by a State to do a different thing. In this age of conglomerates it may be difficult to know what exactly they were chartered to do, but basically the charter is economic, not political. A corporation is not the equivalent of the Democratic party or the Republican party or any other party. In the majority decision in *Bellotti,* Powell says that it is not the right of the corporation to have just the same freedom of speech as the individual person; rather it is the public's need to hear other views or information that warrants the corporation's right to express its views.

Can newspapers say anything they want while Mobil is restricted to producing oil? It isn't that simple. A corporation has a certain degree of freedom; certainly all corporate executives do. They are citizens. Whether they use stockholders' money or not is another matter.

I have a measure of sympathy with Chief Justice Burger's strong implication that media corporations have too much power and that the people who control them have too much power to pursue their own interests. I gave you a horrible example of somebody who hated the President and wanted to smear him on the front page with the help of a former national reporter, but the same thing could be said on the editorial page.

Should publishers have that much power? That bears on the whole issue of professionalism and on the separation of business from the news side. That is an unsolved question.

The issue to worry about is press monopoly. Today there are very few cities left with more than one newspaper. Ninety-odd percent of all towns and cities have only one newspaper. Something like 55-60% of all newspapers in America today are owned by newspaper chains and the proportion is growing. This is a danger. The networks also constitute a kind of danger. I clearly don't want corporate monopoly over channels of information and opinion, but I don't want media monopoly either.

Question for Mr. Warner:

Since most corporate speech writers are drawn from the ranks of the advertising, PR, and journalism professions, how can you ensure that your public messages are built on a sound economic base and truly reflect an understanding of business?

We have four or five writers in our government-public relations department who write speeches and do most of those ads. Once the concept of an ad is devised — and anyone in the company can offer an idea for an ad — we turn it over to a writer to try to put it down. This may be done in 5, 6, 7, or 8 drafts. Then that ad goes to a whole variety of people in the company — to our economists, to our planning people. If it happens to be about the exploration end of our business, for example, it goes to the exploration side. There is no ad that we print that is not looked at either by myself or Mr. Tavoulareas, our president. We do this because we want to avoid exactly what you are getting at, which is a nice, slick, public relations approach to an advertisement. Believe me, these ads are no good to us unless they reflect the views of the management of the company.

Question for Mr. Silk:

If Mobil used its money to buy a newspaper, would you object?

It does give me a certain amount of difficulty. ARCO, as you know, has bought *The London Observer*. Recently, Thornton Bradshaw of ARCO was at our luncheon table at *The New York*

Times. We asked him if he thought oil companies should own newspapers and he replied, "No." "How come ARCO has acquired *The London Observer?*," we asked. "Well," he said, "it was just one of those things. We knew that the paper was in trouble and we thought we would do a good thing. *The Observer* itself is financially unimportant to us; it does not even show on our balance sheet. We just did it." We replied, "If you don't think oil companies should own newspapers, how come you are willing to do it?" His answer was, "We know ourselves."

Mobil, I am sure, knows itself, but I agree with Mr. Bradshaw. People should tend to their own knitting. A corporation that is — I don't mean this in a pejorative sense — a special interest-group producing oil or manufacturing automobiles, for example, should do what it is designed to do. The control of broad public-interest institutions by such a corporation will either corrupt them or raise questions about the institution's credibility.